The Ultimate Roasting Tin Cookbook

Quick and Delicious One Dish Recipes for the Whole Family incl. Desserts, Vegan and Vegetarian Recipes

Barbara Moore

TABLE OF CONTENTS

Why One Dish?

It seems a lifetime ago that the kitchen was the woman's domain where she would spend a large proportion of her day preparing complex meals for the whole family. Today, we're all busier than ever before. Making dinner isn't only the responsibility of the woman of the house – in many households everyone takes their turn to get the food on the table!

Modern life moves at a hectic pace. Working hours are longer than ever, and families are often rushing around trying to get everything done from household chores to taking the kids to extracurricular activities. It all leaves very little time to dedicate to cooking.

So, how can today's busy families come up with speedy yet delicious family meals that everyone will enjoy without having to spend hours sweating over a hot stove?

With less and less time available in which to prepare food, more families are turning to pre-prepared ready meals or takeout fast food. As a result, obesity levels are on the rise and children are growing up unhealthier than ever before. Luckily, there's a solution to this problem that allows you to create and prepare a host of exciting, tasty and yet incredibly simple evening meals for even the pickiest of family members without having to spend hours stirring, blending and mixing.

So, what is the answer?

The answer lies in the humble roasting tin! Something that has been a kitchen staple for generations but that has never been used to its full potential until now.

There's never been a more convenient way to cook than by harnessing the power of the simple roasting tin. A one-size-fits-all solution to preparing everything from meat and fish classics to tasty vegetarian dishes and even snacks and desserts, the roasting tin should be the number one cooking vessel in any modern kitchen. Making it a breeze to whip up a wide variety of both traditional and unusual dinners, it can make preparing your family's suppers a considerably less tedious and time consuming chore.

The concept of this cookbook is an easy one – simply spend a few minutes preparing the ingredients when you get home from work, throw them into your favorite roasting pan or tin and let your oven take the strain! Gone are the days when you needed to stir endless sauces, or prepare different components separately. Armed with these tasty recipes, you can prepare family-friendly meals in minutes, leaving them in your oven cooking while you get on with enjoying some quality time – something that is all too precious in these hectic times!

So, are you ready to find out more about how you can prepare family meals quickly and easily with a single dish? Then read on and discover everything you need to know!

What Is A Roasting Tin?

The first thing that we need to clarify before we go any further is the definition of a roasting tin. It may sound obvious, but in fact there are a few misconceptions about what a roasting tin actually is.

Many people think that a roasting tin (or pan) and a baking dish are the same thing. In fact, they aren't. Nevertheless, they can often be used interchangeably, since in some cases each can perform the function of the other. The difference is more down to tradition and custom than anything physical, but there are a few generalizations that you need to bear in mind.

The Standard Roasting Tin

Sometimes known as a roasting pan, a roasting tin is always made from a durable material that is capable of withstanding some serious scrubbing. This is because the proteins and juices from roast meats cook onto the pan and are hard to remove. For this reason, most roasting tins are made from aluminum or other metals, but sometimes they may be ceramic or glass.

A roasting tin is designed to be big enough and deep enough to hold a turkey or large joint, and therefore, their sides are generally 2.5 – 3" in height so the cooking juices can be easily contained without spilling out all over the oven. Many roasting tins also feature indented bottoms or have included racks so the roast can be held above the juices that come out of the meat during the cooking process.

Roasting tins are staples in the majority of kitchens. It makes it more convenient to roast a turkey and if you're cooking whole chickens, or pork or beef roasts, they're indispensable. Thanks to their special design, they can cook large cuts of meat evenly, trapping the juices beneath. However, if you do not happen to own one, don't panic. You can still prepare the recipes in this book using a baking dish.

The Standard Baking Dish

Although baking dishes are similar to roasting tins, they aren't the same thing. For a start, their shape and size is more flexible than those of a roasting tin. Also, they're traditional made from ceramic materials or glass, although sometimes enameled cast iron or other materials may be used.

A baking dish can be oblong, square or round, and may be either deep or shallow, however the sides are generally only around 1 – 2" in height. Many will also come with their own matching lid making them suitable for use in your refrigerator or oven.

What Are The Differences Between The Two?

Roasting tins:

- Come in different sizes, but all are large enough to accommodate a joint that can feed a small family
- Come with a rack
- Have no lid
- Usually have a non-stick coating of polymer or enamel

Baking dishes:

- Come in varying sizes, but are often smaller than a roasting tin
- Have no rack
- Usually come with a lid

How Are Baking Dishes And Roasting Tins Used?

Primarily, a roasting tin is used (as you can guess from the name) for roasting foods. Yet, there's nothing to stop you from using one as an extra-large baking dish for preparing a large side dish, casserole or cake. If your tin didn't come with its over cover, you can use aluminum foil to cover it whenever necessary.

A baking dish can be used for even more purposes. The smallest sizes can be used as a ramekin for serving crème brulee while the largest sizes are perfect for making casseroles. Typically, they heat up more rapidly than metal roasting tins, and can hold heat better. They also, importantly, can be used to roast meat.

Can I Use Either A Roasting Tin Or Baking Dish For These Recipes?

The purpose for which we've created this cookbook is to assist you in making one dish meals that are swift, tasty and convenient. For a lot of these recipes, it's possible to use either a roasting tin or a baking dish to prepare the ingredients involved and to cook them quickly and easily. One element that you need to keep in mind, though, is that if you will be roasting a joint you will usually need to use a roasting pan that has a rack since the juices will run down into the base of the dish which could then potentially ruin any other ingredients cooking in the tray.

Now that you know the differences between a baking dish and a roasting tin and you understand their uses, it's time to start cooking.

Which Ingredients Do I Need To Prepare For Roasting Tin Recipes?

Although all the single roasting tin recipes that we recommend in this book require a host of different ingredients, there are some store cupboard staples that you'll definitely need to get started. Having a properly-stocked pantry is always the first step to preparing a cooking healthy and tasty meals, and we use some of these key ingredients in the recipes that we've suggested. So, here are a few key items to stock up on the next time you're in the supermarket.

- Canned tomatoes
- Dried spices
- Dried herbs
- Salt and pepper
- Vegetable/sunflower oils
- Pasta
- Onions
- Canned pulses like chickpeas, butter beans and cannellini beans
- Lentils
- Rice
- Couscous
- Bulgur wheat
- Ready to roll pastry
- Potatoes

- Frozen peas
- Eggs
- Milk
- Natural yogurt

With these basics ready to go, you just need to pick up a handful of fresh ingredients to prepare these tasty dinners.

What Kind Of Recipes Can Be Prepared In A Roasting Tin?

Before we get started, you need to know what kind of recipes you'll be able to make using just a roasting tin. We're certain you're going to be surprised!

If you thought roasting tins were solely of use for roasting meat, it's time to think again! Yes, of course you can prepare a whole chicken, turkey or joint of pork or beef in your roasting tin. However, there are endless other options available that will guarantee you a different kind of meal every day of the week, all without the hassle of extra washing up!

Perhaps you're looking for classic meat recipes for a traditionally family dinner? Or maybe you're keen to ring the changes with a meat-based meal that takes its inspiration from exotic cuisines?

Maybe you're seeking a healthy yet convenient dinner that will satisfy your hunger but not pile on the pounds? Or maybe you're trying to add more fish and seafood into your diet but aren't sure how to get started?

You may even be feeding vegetarians or vegans and need inspiration for simple but satisfying entrees that use only plant-based ingredients. Or how about an easier way of making delicious snacks and sumptuous desserts to round off any meal?

Rest assured that we've got recipes that cover all of these possibilities in this handy cookbook. So put your apron on, wash your hands and choose the perfect recipe to delight your family this evening!

Meat Roasting Tin Recipes

When you think about roasting tins, you probably automatically think of meat dishes. After all, roasting tins were designed for cooking joints, whole birds and cuts of meat.

While roasting tins are a helpful kitchen accessory when you need to beautifully and evenly cook a whole joint or bird, they can equally be used to cook smaller cuts of meat.

That's why we've written this chapter. It's designed to help you discover the simplest and most convenient ways to prepare meat-based meals in a single roasting tin that are sure to delight the whole family.

Whether you need an easy and speedy midweek dinner, or whether you're looking for something that's sure to impress your dinner party guests, we've got a meat roasting tin recipe to delight you.

Garlic And Rosemary Roast Lamb With Olives And Artichokes

The first recipe that we're going to look at in this chapter is a traditional classic that's perfect for a Sunday lunch. Delivering on every front, the olives, artichokes, garlic and rosemary all work perfectly together to enhance the lamb's flavor, and the addition of cannellini beans serves to soak up even more wonderful flavor from juices of the meat. Whether you're entertaining friends or family or just want to treat yourself, you're sure to find this an ideal meal.

This recipe can easily be prepared in advanced. Just pop all the various ingredients into a tin then pop it into your refrigerator. Remove it 15 minutes before the time comes to begin cooking and you're good to go!

> Serves Four
>
> Preparation time:10 minutes
>
> Cooking time: 25 minutes
>
> Total time: 35 minutes

Ingredients

- 350g//1 ½ cups vine cherry tomatoes
- A jar of drained artichokes with a tablespoon of oil reserved from the jar
- 180g//1 cup of black pitted olives
- 8 lamb chops
- 2 sprigs of chopped rosemary leaves

- ◆ 1 teaspoon sea salt
- ◆ 2 crushed garlic cloves
- ◆ Juice of a lemon
- ◆ 1 tin of drained cannellini beans
- ◆ A handful of chopped flat-leaf parsley or basil

Instructions

1. Preheat your oven to 180C//350F
2. Put the vine charry tomatoes into your roasting tin together with the artichokes
3. Rub the oil from the artichoke jar over the lamb chops
4. Scatter the garlic, salt and rosemary across the top
5. Put the chops into the roasting tin
6. Put the tin into your oven
7. Cook for 25 minutes
8. Stir the juice of the lemon and the cannellini beans through the olives and tomatoes
9. Leave the lamb chops for five minutes to rest
10. Scatter the parsley or basil over the top
11. Serve hot

Peanut Chilli Beef With Sweetcorn, Spring Onions And Red Bell Peppers

If you're a fan of stir fry and exotic oriental flavors, you're sure to love this delicious roasting tin recipe. You won't even need to stand in front of the hot stove top and stir! It's no wonder that this is such a popular choice since the peppers, beef and sweetcorn all cook perfectly in your oven while the peanut-soy dressing adds a wonderful kick that makes this a more-ish dinner that you won't want to wait to prepare again!

When you need a fast and simple weekday dinner that is rich in flavor, don't hesitate to get out your roasting tin and whip up this Asian-inspired meal.

> Serves Two
> Preparation time: 10 minutes
> Cooking time: 25 minutes
> Total time: 35minutes

Ingredients

- 400g//16oz rump steak cut into 1.5cm// ½" slices
- 200g//8oz green beans
- 175g//1 cup baby sweetcorn

- 1 finely sliced red bell pepper
- 1 finely grated red chilli
- 2 finely grated garlic cloves

- 5cm//2"fresh ginger that has been grated
- 1 teaspoon sea salt
- A tablespoon of sesame oil
- 3 tablespoons of crunchy peanut butter
- 1 tablespoon of dark soy sauce
- 1 tablespoon of rice vinegar
- A tablespoon of water
- 50g//1 ½ cups of chopped spinach
- 3 finely sliced spring onions
- A handful of chopped salted peanuts
- Rice or noodles

Instructions

1 Preheat your oven to 200C//400F

2 Put the steak, sweetcorn, bell pepper and green beans in a roasting tin in a single layer

3 Add the sesame oil, sea salt, ginger, garlic and grated chilli

4 Mix well to coat everything

5 Move the steak slices to the top so they char

6 Put the tin into the oven

7 Cook for 25 minutes

8 Meanwhile, mix together the rice vinegar, soy sauce, water and peanut butter

9 Once the steak has cooked, stir the spinach through

10 Pour the prepared dressing across the top

11 Scatter the salted peanuts and spring onions across the top

12 Serve alongside rice or cooked noodles

Sausage Bake With Cherry Tomatoes And Long-Stem Broccoli

This sausage bake works perfectly with the fresh flavors of broccoli, tomatoes and courgettes and this results in a light meal that is ideal after a long day at work. Ideal in summer or winter, this delicious meal is the perfect comfort food when served with mashed potato or is a great summer supper when served with slices of crusty bread or a green salad.

Serves 2
Preparation time – 10 minutes
Cooking time – 30 minutes
Total time – 40 minutes

Ingredients

- 250g//1 ½ cups tenderstem broccoli
- 500g//3 cup sliced courgettes
- 300g//1 ½ cups vine cherry tomatoes
- 1 ½ tablespoons of olive oil
- 2 crushed garlic cloves
- 3 fresh rosemary sprigs
- 1 teaspoon of sea salt
- A teaspoon of chilli flakes
- 8 chipolata sausages
- Juice of 1 lemon

Instructions

1. Preheat your oven to 230C//450F
2. Put the tenderstem broccoli in a bowl
3. Pour boiling water over the broccoli
4. Allow to stand for one minute
5. Drain the broccoli
6. Put all of the ingredients into a large roasting tin in a single layer
7. Mix together the ingredients well
8. Ensure the sausages are lying on the top
9. Put the tin into the oven
10. Cook for 30 minutes
11. Scatter sea salt and squeeze the lemon juice over your vegetables
12. Serve hot

Spicy Roast Chicken With Onion, Aubergine And Peppers

Chicken lends itself perfectly to single roasting tin recipes, and whether you're preparing a casual meal to enjoy with friends or a simple family dinner, this spicy roast chicken recipe is ideal. While this dish is warming thanks to the Middle Eastern spices used, it isn't hot, so it's great for children and those who don't enjoy chillis.

This is also a beautiful dish that looks colorful when you bring it to the table, and with its wholesome ingredients, it's sure to be a hit at any mealtime.

> Serves 4
> Preparation time – 10 minutes
> Cooking time – 30 minutes
> Total time – 40 minutes

Ingredients

- 1 aubergine cut up into cubes
- 2 sliced red peppers
- 1 sliced yellow bell pepper
- 1 red onion, cut in slices
- 4 quartered vine tomatoes
- 3 garlic cloves
- 4 teaspoons of ras-el-hanout
- 2 tablespoons of olive oil
- A teaspoon of sea salt
- 4 chicken breasts

- ◆ A handful of fresh coriander
- ◆ Natural yogurt
- ◆ Flatbread or couscous to serve

Instructions

1. Preheat your oven to 200C//400F
2. Put the yellow and red peppers, aubergine, tomatoes, cloves of garlic and the slices of red onion into a roasting tin
3. Add two teaspoons of ras-el-hanout
4. Add one tablespoon of olive oil
5. Sprinkle on the sea salt
6. Mix well (your hands are the best way to do this)
7. Put the chicken onto the vegetables
8. Drizzle the remainder of the oil over
9. Add the salt together with the rest of the ras-el-hanout
10. Put the tin in the oven
11. Cook for 30 minutes
12. Serve with a scoop of yogurt, couscous and flatbreads

Chicken, Chorizo And Leek Pie

You may never have thought of making a pie in your trusty roasting tin, but believe it or not, it's perfectly possible! This hearty pie is an ideal midweek dinner when served hot, or is just as delicious served cold with salad for a simple lunch. Easy to make and tasty to eat, it's sure to tick all your boxes when you want comfort food with flavor.

Serves 4

Preparation time – 10 minutes

Cooking time – 30 minutes

Total time – 40 minutes

Ingredients

- 2 sliced leeks
- 4 chicken breasts cut into chunks
- 120g// ½ cup diced chorizo
- 300g//1 ¼ cups crème fraiche
- Juice and the zest of ½ a lemon
- 1 teaspoon of sea salt
- Black pepper
- 1 beaten egg
- 1 sheet of ready-rolled puff pastry

Instructions

1 Preheat your oven to 200C//400F

2 Put the sliced leeks into a bowl

3 Cover with some boiling water

4 Allow to steep for two minutes

5 Use a colander to drain the leeks

6 Put the drained leeks into your roasting tin

7 Add the chorizo, chicken, crème fraiche, salt, lemon juice and zest, and a few grinds of black pepper

8 Mix well

9 Brush the roasting tin's edges with beaten egg

Put the pastry over the top of the ingredients

1 Press the pastry's edges with a fork against the tin's edges

2 Brush the pastry with beaten egg

3 Cut across the center of the pie so the steam can escape

4 Put the tin in the oven

5 Cook for 30 minutes

6 Allow to rest for around five minutes

7 Serve hot

Meatball Cassoulet

This French-style rustic stew is a simple but delicious evening meal for all the family to enjoy. This hearty dish combines ready-made meatballs with white beans for a filling and satisfying entrée. Serve with crusty bread to mop up the delicious flavors for an even more comforting workday dinner.

Serves 4

Preparation time – 25 minutes

Cooking time – 2 hours

Total time – 2 hours 25 minutes

Ingredients

- 2 cans of white beans
- 500ml//2 cups of tomato juice
- 400g//14 oz frozen ready-cooked meatballs
- 50g//1 cup diced carrot
- 50g//1 cup diced onion
- 50g//1 cup diced celery
- 1 tablespoon of Worcestershire sauce
- ½ teaspoon of dried basil
- ½ teaspoon of dried oregano
- ½ teaspoon of dried paprika

Instructions

1. Preheat the oven 150C//300F
2. Add all of the ingredients to the roasting tin
3. Mix well to thoroughly combine
4. Put the tin into the oven
5. Cook for 2 hours
6. Serve hot alongside some crusty bread to soak up the juices

Fish And Seafood Roasting Tin Recipes

If you thought that fish or seafood were difficult or time-consuming to prepare and cook, it's time to think again. These tasty and simple recipes will change your mind completely!

You may never have considered cooking salmon, cod, scallops or other seafood in a roasting tin, but actually, you'll be surprised by how well it works. It gives you the opportunity to add a host of delicious flavors to these healthy sources of protein as a midweek meal that's low calorie yet full of taste.

Roasted Broccoli And Salmon With Chilli, Garlic, Ginger And Lime

This Asian inspired recipe is the ideal choice if you're looking for a tasty fish dish to serve your family. Perfect for any occasion, this simple roasting tin recipe is the ultimate easy dinner. Thanks to the lime, peanut and ginger dressing, you're sure to make this a family favorite.

The punchy dressing is packed with coriander, lime, peanuts and fish sauce for a delicious Thai flavor. It works perfectly with the salmon, and the peanuts add a crunchy texture. As the broccoli and salmon are cooking it's a breeze to put the tasty dressing together so your meal can be on the table in no time.

Serves 4

Preparation time –10 minutes

Cooking time – 15 minutes

Total time – 25 minutes

Ingredients

- 400g//2 cups broccoli florets
- 2 grated garlic cloves
- 2 tablespoons of sesame oil

- 4 salmon fillets
- 2 chopped spring onions
- 2.5cm//1 inch grated ginger
- 1 finely sliced red chilli

- 2 tablespoons fish sauce
- 4 tablespoons vegetable oil
- The juice and zest of 2 limes
- 30g//¼ cup chopped fresh coriander
- 50g//1/4 cup chopped peanuts

Instructions

1. Preheat your oven to 200C//400F
2. Put the broccoli into a roasting tin
3. Scatter grated garlic over the top
4. Pour the sesame oil over the broccoli and toss it well
5. Put the salmon into the tin with the broccoli
6. Cover up with foil tightly
7. Put the tin in the oven
8. Bake for 25 minutes until the salmon is cooked to your preference
9. While the salmon is cooking, mix the chilli, ginger, spring onions, vegetable oil, fish sauce, lime juice, lime zest, peanuts and coriander together
10. Take the cooked broccoli and salmon out of the oven
11. Cover the salmon generously with its dressing
12. Drizzle the rest of the dressing across the broccoli
13. Serve immediately

CRISP BAKED COD WITH BEANS, PEAS AND HERBED BROCCOLI

This delicious crisp baked cod dish is perfect for weeknights when you don't have much time or energy left to prepare a complex dinner. The ingredients used here are all store-cupboard staples – frozen peas, breadcrumbs, pesto and butter beans, so they're simple to get your hands on. All of the delicious flavors from the tin are soaked into the beans making this a comforting and tasty treat at the end of a long day. Serve this dish with some crusty bread and it's even more delicious and satisfying

Serves 2

Preparation Time – 10 minutes

Cooking Time – 25 minutes

Total Time – 35 minutes

INGREDIENTS

- 300g//1 ¼ cups tenderstem broccoli
- 300g//1 ¼ cups frozen peas
- 2 sliced courgettes
- 2 tablespoons of olive oil
- 1 teaspoon of sea salt
- Black pepper to taste
- 4 fillets of cod
- 4 teaspoons of green pesto
- 4 tablespoons of breadcrumbs

- ◆ 1 tin of drained butter beans
- ◆ Juice and zest of half a lemon
- ◆ 1 largebunch of finely choppedbasil leaves

INSTRUCTIONS

1 Preheat your oven to 200C//400F

2 Put the tenderstem broccoli into a bowl and cover it with boiling water

3 Allow it to rest for two minutes

4 Drain well

5 Mix the courgettes, frozen peas and broccoli in a roasting pan together with 1 ½ tablespoons of olive oil, a few grinds of black pepper and a sprinkle of sea salt.

6 Place the cod over the vegetables

7 Spread a teaspoon of pesto over each one

8 Scatter breadcrumbs over the top

9 Drizzle with the remainder of the olive oil

10 Grind black pepper over the top

11 Put in the oven

12 Cook for 25 minutes

13 Remove the tin from your oven

Stir the butter beans into the cooked ingredients

1. Add lemon juice and zest
2. Add the fresh basil
3. Serve hot

Scallop, Chorizo And Leek Gratin

If you need an easy and delicious way of preparing scallops, this one roasting tin dish is an ideal choice. You may be nervous about cooking scallops since they aren't the most traditional of ingredients, yet with the creamy leaks and punchy chorizo in this simple dish, you're sure to be impressed by how convenient this meal is to cook and serve. Whether you're trying to delight a date or please the family, this gratin won't disappoint.

Serves 2
Preparation time – 10 minutes
Cooking time – 25 minutes
Total time – 35 minutes

Ingredients

- 1 large sliced leek
- 1 teaspoon of sea salt
- Ground black pepper
- 300g//10 ½ oz scallops
- 75g//3oz chopped chorizo
- 250ml//1 cup double cream
- A handful of chopped parsley
- 50g//1 cup breadcrumbs
- 30g// ¼ cup of grated parmesan
- Zest of half a lemon
- 1 tablespoon olive oil

Instructions

1. Preheat your oven to 200C//400F
2. Put the leeks in a bowl and cover with boiling water
3. Allow it to sit and rest for two minutes
4. Drain well
5. Put the leeks in a roasting tin
6. Season week with flakes of sea salt and a few grinds of black pepper
7. Place the scallops onto the leeks
8. Scatter the chorizo over the top
9. Pour the cream over everything evenly
10. Mix the parsley, parmesan, the zest of the lemon and the breadcrumbs together
11. Scatter this on top of the dish
12. Drizzle a little olive oil across the top
13. Put into the oven
14. Cook for 25 minutes
15. Leave for five minutes to allow the dish to cool
16. Serve hot with crusty bread

Keralan Prawn Curry

Whether prepared fresh and served hot or whether cooked in advance and then frozen for a later meal, this Keralan prawn curry is packed with Asian flavors like turmeric and coconut and offers you all of the exotic appeal of India without having to spend hours slaving over the stove. Made in a single roasting tin, this aromatic curry will set your tastebuds tingling, especially when served with naan bread and basmati rice.

Prepared using primarily store cupboard ingredients, it's the ideal choice for any busy weeknight. You can make the cooking process even swifter by using frozen prawns defrosted in cold running water when you choose this user-friendly midweek dinner.

> Serves 2
> Preparation Time – 10 minutes
> Cooking Time – 30 minutes
> Total Time – 40 minutes

Ingredients

- 220g//1 ¼ cups halved vine cherry tomatoes
- 1 sliced green pepper
- 1 sliced onion
- 2cm/1" grated fresh ginger
- 2 teaspoons of mustard seeds

- 1 teaspoon of black pepper
- 1 teaspoon of ground coriander
- 1 teaspoon of ground cumin
- ½ teaspoon of ground turmeric
- 1teaspoon of ground chilli
- A few curry leaves
- 1 teaspoon of sea salt
- 1 tablespoon of oil
- 1 can of coconut milk
- 325g//1 cup king prawns
- 100g//3 ¼ cups chopped spinach
- Juice of 1 lime
- A large handful of coriander
- 1 chopped red chilli

Instructions

1. Preheat your oven to 200C//400

2. Put the tomatoes, green pepper, ginger, onion, salt, oil and spices into your roasting tin

3. Mix well so everything is evenly coated

4. Put the tin into the oven

5. Cook for 20 minutes

6. Take all the vines off the tomatoes

7. Squash the tomatoes down

8. Add the prawns, spinach and the coconut milk

9. Put the tin back into your oven for 10 minutes

10. Remove from the oven

11. Season with the sea salt and the lime juice

12. Scatter the chilli and coriander over the top

13. Serve with some basmati rice and some naan breads

Curried Fish And Lentil Dhal

This tasty fish curry is full of Eastern flavor and represents a wonderful dish for curry night. The ideal alternative to chicken or beef dishes, the lentil dhal adds protein and fiber while the fish adds texture and taste. The result is an exotic family pleasing recipe that won't fail to bring an unusual twist to traditional midweek meals.

> Serves 2
> Preparation time – 20 minutes
> Cooking time – 1 hour plus marinating time
> Total time – 1 hour 20 minutes

Ingredients

- 2 chopped onions
- 1 tablespoon of grated ginger
- 1 tablespoon of sunflower oil
- 2 1/2 tablespoons of mild curry powder
- 1 teaspoon of brown mustard seeds
- 1 ½ teaspoons of nigella seeds
- 85g// ½ cup red lentils
- 85g// ½ cup split peas
- 1 ¼ teaspoons ground turmeric
- 1 can of coconut milk
- 3 tablespoons of natural yoghurt
- 2 cod fillets

- ◆ 2 diced plum tomatoes
- ◆ Juice of a fresh lime
- ◆ A lime cut into wedges for serving
- ◆ A small handful of fresh coriander leaves
- ◆ 2 tablespoons of crispy onions
- ◆ Mango chutney and a warm naan bread to serve

INSTRUCTIONS

1. Preheat your oven to 200C//400F
2. Mix the ginger, onions, oil, curry powder, mustard seeds and a teaspoon of nigella seeds with 5 tablespoons of water in the roasting tin
3. Cook for around 15 minutes
4. Sir the lentils, a teaspoon of the turmeric, split peas,the coconut milk and half a can of water into the tin
5. Put the tin back in the oven
6. Cook for 30 minutes
7. Meanwhile, mix the rest of the turmeric, curry powder, and nigella seeds with the yogurt.
8. Rub the flavored yogurt over the cod fillets
9. Allow to marinate in your refrigerator while you cook the lentils
10. Stir the dhal

11 Mix all of the lime juice, a teaspoon of salt, and tomatoes into the dhal

12 Place the cod on top

13 Sprink on some seasoning

14 Put the tin into the oven

15 Cook for 15 minutes

16 Scatter the crispy onions and coriander over the top

17 Serve with lime wedges, yogurt, mango chutney and naan bread

Salmon And Roasted Asparagus

This simple yet sophisticated dish is an ideal date night dinner that is certain to impress that special someone. Made using a few easy ingredients, this is a weekend or weeknight meal that is full of rich flavors. So user-friendly that even a complete beginner could prepare it, this one roasting tin recipe is ideal for any occasion.

Serves 2

Preparation time – 20 minutes

Cooking time – 50 minutes

Total time – 1 hour and 10 minutes

Ingredients

◆ 400g//3 cups of new potatoes

◆ 2 tablespoons of olive oil

◆ 8 halved and trimmed asparagus spears

◆ 2 handfuls of small cherry tomatoes

◆ 1 tablespoon of balsamic vinegar

◆ 2 salmon fillets

◆ A handful of fresh basil leaves

Instructions

1 Preheat your oven to 200C//400F
2 Put the potatoes and a tablespoon of the olive oil into your roasting tin
3 Cook for 20 minutes
4 Add the asparagus spears to the potatoes
5 Return to your oven and cook for 15 minutes
6 Add the vinegar together with the cherry tomatoes to the tin
7 Place the fillets of salmon on the vegetables
8 Drizzle the rest of the oil over the tin
9 Put back in the oven
10 Cook for 15 minutes
11 Scatter the basil over the top
12 Serve hot

Vegetarian Roasting Tin Dishes

Perhaps you're trying out the vegetarian lifestyle for yourself. Or maybe you're preparing a meal for a vegetarian friend or family member and are seeking inspiration for easy yet delicious dishes to make that are sure to impress? Either way, this chapter can help you out.

The vegetarian diet is becoming more popular these days with more people recognizing the health benefits that come along with a plant-based diet. Introducing more plant-based meals into our lives can help us to stave off a host of diseases and illnesses that are associated with eating a lot of red meat.

However, it isn't always easy to think of new and exciting ways of making vegetable-based meals for each day of your week. We all know some of the classics – vegetable lasagne, lentil curry, or nut roast. Yet, there's only so far that those staples can take us. Luckily, there are lots of ways to combine delicious vegetarian ingredients with amazing flavors to create healthy meals that will tickle your tastebuds.

Roast Tomatoes And Red Peppers With Bulgur Wheat, Pine Nuts And Feta Cheese

If you're looking for a vegetarian recipe that is an easy and swift summer midweek dinner for all the family, this tasty bulgur wheat-based dish is sure to satisfy. Packed with delicious Mediterranean flavor, it's sure to tantalize your tastebuds.

The roast peppers and tomatoes create their very own dressing to complement this speedy bulgur wheat hot salad, but if you want a little more flavor you can add a touch of lemon juice for an extra citrus kick. Should you prefer the roast red peppers to be more charred and less crunchy, feel free to cook them by themselves in your oven for around 15 minutes before you add the garlic and cherry tomatoes.

```
Serves 4
Preparation time – 5 minutes
Cooking time – 35 minutes
Total time – 40 minutes
```

Ingredients

- 2 red bell peppers (chopped up in chunks)
- 300g//1 ½ cups of cherry tomatoes
- 4 cloves of garlic with the skin remaining on
- 2 tablespoons of olive oil
- 40g//1/3 cup of pine nuts

- Black pepper and flakes of sea salt to taste
- 200g//1 cup bulgur wheat
- 400ml//1 ¾ cups of vegetable stock
- 100g//1/2 cup feta cheese
- Basil or flat leaf parsley for garnishing

Instructions

1. Preheat the oven to 200C//400F
2. Put the cherry tomatoes, the garlic cloves and the chopped red bell peppers into a roasting tin
3. Drizzle olive oil over the vegetables
4. Scatter black pepper and sea salt over the top
5. Put in your oven for 15 minutes to roast
6. Remove from your oven and scatter pine nuts over the top
7. Put the tray back in the oven for 5 minutes more
8. Add the bulgur wheat to the tin
9. Stir it gently through the tomatoes and peppers
10. Pour in the stock
11. Mix well to submerge the bulgur wheat
12. Cover the tin tightly with tin foil

13 Return the tray to your oven for around 15 minutes

14 Remove from the oven

15 Take off the tin foil

16 Scatter the herbs and the feta cheese across the hot salad

17 Season with grinds of black pepper and some sea salt to taste

18 Serve hot

Chipotle Roast Sweetcorn With Black Beans, Lime, Feta And Squash

If you're looking for a Mexican inspired meal that's suited to vegetarians, this chipotle roast sweetcorn dish is the ideal choice. Taking a combination of store cupboard staples and fresh ingredients, this south of the border dinner brings all of the tastes of summer to your table. Easy and quick to make in a single roasting tin, it's a wonderful busy weeknight option, with bright textures and colors. Serve it with rice, alone or with other Mexican dishes as part of a sharing feast.

Serves 4

Preparation time – 10 minutes

Cooking time – 45 minutes

Total time – 55 minutes

Ingredients

- 750g//6 cups of sliced squash
- 4 whole sweetcorn
- 1 can of drained black beans
- 1 teaspoon of chipotle chilli flakes
- 1 teaspoon of ground coriander
- A teaspoon of salt
- 1 teaspoon of ground cumin
- 2 tablespoons of olive oil
- 200g//2 cups of crumbled feta cheese
- Juice of a lime
- 25g// ½ cup chopped coriander

- 2 finely chopped spring onions
- 4 heaped tablespoons of sour cream
- Rice to serve

Instructions

1. Preheat your oven to 200c//400F
2. Mix the sweetcorn, black beans and squash together in your roasting tin
3. Add the olive oil, the salt and the spices
4. Put the tin into the oven
5. Cook for 45 minutes
6. Remove from the oven
7. Squeeze the lime juice over the dish
8. Scatter the feta cheese, the spring onions and the coriander over the top
9. Serve with sour cream and rice

Mini Stuffed Pumpkins With Goat's Cheese And Sage

When it comes to the winter months, finding the ultimate comfort food is just important when feeding vegetarians as for meat eaters. This warming dish is the ideal choice. Even the most hardened meat eater is sure to love this beautiful dinner that is ideal for the cold winter evenings. As pretty as it is delicious, you're sure to impress anyone that you serve this to.

Serves 4

Preparation time – 10 minutes

Cooking time – 1 hour

Total time – 1 hour 10 minutes

Ingredients

- 4 mini pumpkins
- Sea salt
- 16 leaves of fresh sage
- 2 teaspoons of chilli flakes
- 250g//2 cups of goat's cheese
- ½ teaspoon of chilli powder
- 2 ½ tablespoons of olive oil

Instructions

1 Preheat your oven to 200C//400F

2 Slice off each pumpkin's top carefully

3 Use a small but sharp knife to cut around the central cavity where the seeds are

4 Scoop out the seeds using a spoon

5 Set the seeds aside

6 Season inside each cavity with sea salt

7 Line the cavity with sage leaves

8 Stuff each pumpkin with goat's cheese

9 Scatter chilli flakes over the top

10 Replace the pumpkin lid

11 Rub each with half a tablespoon of the olive oil

12 Scatter salt over the top

13 Top the pumpkins with sage leaves

14 Put the tin into the oven

15 Cook for 1 hour

16 Use a sheet of kitchen paper to rub the seeds to remove any remaining flesh

17 Toss the seeds with half a tablespoon of olive oil, the sea salt and the chilli powder

18 Ten minutes before the pumpkins are cooked, add the seeds to the tin

19 Return the tin to the oven

20 Serve whole with a green salad

Broccoli, Chilli, Walnut And Gorgonzola Quiche

If you never thought about cooking a quiche in a roasting tin, this is the ideal recipe to test it out! Easy and quick, this quiche is the ideal packed lunch or picnic treat, or why not serve it with a salad for a tasty and speedy dinner? With its puff pastry base, this quiche feels wonderfully indulgent, yet it's a breeze to put together. The gorgonzola and broccoli beautifully complement each other, while the chilli gives a slight kick that can't be beaten.

Serves 4

Preparation time – 10 minutes

Cooking time – 30 minutes

Total time – 40 minutes

Ingredients

- A ready-rolled sheet of puff pastry
- 300g// 1 ½ cups of halved broccoli florets
- ½ chopped red onion
- 1 teaspoon of chilli flakes
- 125g// 1 cup gorgonzola picante cheese
- 30g// ¼ cup chopped walnuts
- 100ml// ½ cup single cream
- 4 eggs
- Zest of 1 lemon
- 1 teaspoon of sea salt
- 1 crushed clove of garlic

Instructions

1   Preheat your oven to 200C//400F

2   Use baking parchment to line your roasting tin

3   Cover the tin's base with puff pastry – make sure it comes up the sides so the filling stays in

4   Scatter the chilli flakes, red onion, broccoli florets, gorgonzola and walnuts across the puff pastry evenly

5   Beat the eggs, sea salt, garlic and lemon zest with the cream then pour the mix over the cheese and the broccoli

6   Put the tin in the oven

7   Cook for 30 minutes

8   Allow to sit for 10 minutes to cool

9   Serve warm

Gnocchi With Chilli, Roast Peppers, Ricotta And Rosemary

When you've had a hard day at work, the last thing you need is to face making a complex dinner. This family-friendly, simple to prepare, one roasting tin gnocchi dish isn't just suitable for vegetarians, it's sure to delight the carnivores in your family too! The red peppers and ricotta cheese perfectly complement the gnocchi, while the crunchy texture adds extra pleasure to your meal.

Serves 2

Preparation time –15 minutes

Cooking time– 30 minutes

Total time – 45 minutes

Ingredients

- 500g//4 cups gnocchi
- 500g//4 cups of mixed yellow and red chopped peppers
- 2 tablespoons of olive oil
- 200g//1 cup halved cherry tomatoes
- 2 bay leaves
- 2 garlic cloves
- 1 teaspoon of chilli flakes
- 2 fresh rosemary sprigs
- 1 teaspoon of sea salt
- 4 tablespoons of ricotta cheese
- Ground black pepper
- A handful of freshly chopped parsley

Instructions

1 Preheat your oven to 200C//400 F
2 Put the gnocchi in a bowl and cover with some boiling water
3 Allow to stand for two minutes
4 Drain well
5 Put the gnocchi in your roasting tin
6 Add all of the other ingredients save the ricotta cheese
7 Mix all of the ingredients thoroughly and ensure there is only a single layer
8 Transfer the tin to the oven
9 Cook for 30 minutes
10 Season to taste with ground pepper and salt
11 Dollop ricotta cheese on the top
12 Scatter the parsley across the top
13 Serve hot

Roast Courgette, Macaroni And Aubergine Bake

There's nothing quite like a pasta dish, and with this single roasting tin recipe, you won't have to stand and sweat over the stove. Simply pop the ingredients into the tin and allow the oven do the work! Made with delicious fresh ingredients, this is a comforting dish for any winter evening or a tasty summer supper when served with salad. It's ready in less than an hour too, so dinner can be on the table in no time! This is a particularly good recipe to get children to eat vegetables since they're hidden in the tomato-based sauce. Meanwhile, the Boursin cheese adds herb and garlic flavors that save you time without compromising on taste.

Serves 4

Preparation time – 10 minutes

Cooking time – 30 minutes

Total time – 40 minutes

Ingredients

- 1 aubergine, cubed
- 1 sliced courgette
- 1 teaspoon of sea salt
- 3 tablespoons of olive oil
- 300g//1 ½ cups of chopped tomatoes
- 1 block of crumbled Boursin cheese
- 40g//1 cup breadcrumbs

Instructions

1 Preheat your oven to 230C//450F

2 Prepare a pan of salted boiling water

3 Put the courgettes, aubergines, sea salt and a tablespoon of olive oil into a roasting tin

4 Mix well

5 Put the tin into the oven

6 Cook for 10 minutes

7 Meanwhile, cook the pasta in the pan of boiling water for ten minutes

8 Drain the pasta well

9 Remove the roasting tin from the oven

10 Stir the pasta into the courgettes and aubergines

11 Add the chopped tomatoes to the tin along with a tablespoon of oil

12 Turn down your oven to 220C//425F

13 Scatter the Boursin cheese over the top

14 Scatter the breadcrumbs over the dish

15 Drizzle the remaining oil over the top

16 Put the tin in the oven

17 Cook for 20 minutes

18 Allow 5 minutes rest time

19 Serve warm

Halloumi Bake

Simple yet no less delicious, this easy vegetarian traybake mixed roasted vegetables and chickpeas with halloumi cheese for a nutritious and satisfying family meal. Not only is this a colorful dish, it also serves up no less than four of your five a day!

Serves 4
Preparation time – 15 minutes
Cooking time – 1 hour
Total time – 1 hour 15 minutes

Ingredients

- 750g/1 ¼ cups of new potatoes cut in halves
- 4 tablespoons of olive oil
- 2 quartered red onions
- 1 can of drained chickpeas
- 1 sliced red pepper
- ½ a cauliflower cut into florets
- 250g//1 1/3 cupsof cherry tomatoes in mixed colors
- 5 peeled garlic cloves
- 250g//2 cups of sliced halloumi cheese
- A bunch of torn basil leaves

Instructions

1. Preheat the oven to 160C//325F
2. Put the new potatoes into a roasting tin along with the onions
3. Pour two tablespoons of olive oil over the top
4. Put the tin into the oven
5. Cook for 30 minutes
6. Take out of the oven
7. Add the cauliflower, chickpeas, garlic, tomatoes and peppers
8. Drizzle over two tablespoons of oil
9. Put the tin back in your oven
10. Cook for another 25 minutes
11. Briefly toss everything together
12. Put the slices of halloumi cheese on top
13. Return to your oven for 10 minutes
14. Remove from the oven
15. Scatter the basil across the top
16. Serve hot

Vegan Roasting Tin Recipes

The amount of people adopting the vegan lifestyle have increased exponentially over the last few years, with people of all ages embracing this way of living with open arms. Whether for health or moral reasons, choosing to eat only vegan foods presents some issues for those who are unfamiliar with this way of eating.

There are many things that are excluded from the vegan diet. All animal-derived products must be avoided. Obviously, this means no meat or fish. However, it also means many more staple foods are outlawed. Vegans eat no dairy products, so this means no cheese, no milk and no eggs. They also avoid gelatine and honey.

Before you panic and think that there can't possibly be any delicious recipes that are suitable for vegans to eat, the good news is that there are lots of nutritious and tasty foods that are perfectly acceptable. There are also vegan alternatives for cheese, yogurt and milk, so you have an even wider variety of options open to you when it comes to preparing weekend or midweek dinners.

Nevertheless, all of the vegan one roasting tin recipes that we have included in this chapter are all purely plant-based, using only vegetables, nuts, grains and seeds, so you won't have to worry about sourcing alternatives or finding complex ingredients.

Sweet Potato Stew With Tomato And Peanut Sauce

If you need a comforting midweek dinner for vegan friends or family members, or if you're introducing more plant-based meals into your own diet, this tasty stew is filling, satisfying and delicious. It's also very easy and quick to prepare, with the oven doing all the hard work for you. Made using primarily store cupboard staples, this is a convenient option when you can't be bothered to cook!

Serves 4

Preparation time – 10 minutes

Cooking time -1 hour

Total time – 1 hour10 minutes

Ingredients

- 1kg//2 lbs 3 oz peeled and sliced sweet potatoes
- 1 sliced onion
- 2.5cm//1 inch of grated ginger
- 2 crushed garlic cloves
- 1 tablespoon of olive oil
- 1 red chilli
- 1 teaspoon of sea salt
- 50g// ¼ cup of peanut butter
- 1 tin of chopped tomatoes
- 400ml//1 ¾ cups of vegetable stock
- A handful of chopped fresh coriander
- A handful of chopped salted peanuts

Instructions

1. Preheat your oven to 200C//400F

2. Mix the onion, sweet potatoes, the chilli, garlic and the ginger along with the sea salt and the oil in your roasting tin

3. Put the tin in the oven

4. Cook for 45 minutes

5. Meanwhile, mix the peanut butter with the stock and the chopped tomatoes

6. Pour the mix over the roast sweet potatoes

7. Stir well then put back into the oven

8. Cook for 15 minutes

9. Take out the whole chilli

10. Season well with salt to suit your tastes

11. Scatter the chopped peanuts and coriander over the top

12. Serve with rice

Slow Cooked Ratatouille

Is there anything more comforting that a traditional ratatouille recipe? The ultimate choice for a cold winter evening, this oven—baked classic is made with aubergine, courgette, tomatoes and peppers for a speedy and simple supper. The key here is to slice the courgettes extremely thinly. This allows them to thoroughly absorb the flavors of the sauce. Either eat it immediately or serve warm the next day when the flavors have settled.

Serves 4

Preparation time – 10 minutes

Cooking time – 1 hour

Total time – 1 hour 10 minutes

Ingredients

- 2 large and sliced courgettes
- 1 large sliced aubergine
- 2 chopped red peppers
- 2 crushed garlic cloves
- 1 chopped red onion
- 2 tablespoons of olive oil
- Black pepper to taste
- 2 teaspoons of sea salt
- 25g/ ¼ cup of chopped fresh basil
- 2 cans of chopped tomatoes
- 75g//1 ½ cups breadcrumbs

- 30g// ¼ cup grated vegan Parmesan cheese (optional)
- Crusty bread to serve

Instructions

1. Preheat your oven to 200C//400F
2. Mix the garlic, salt, oil, basil and pepper with all the vegetables in your roasting tin
3. Top with the topped tomatoes, smoothing them over the vegetables
4. Put the tin in the oven
5. Cook for 30 minutes
6. Take the tin out of the oven
7. Turn up the heat to 220C//425F
8. Stir the vegetables
9. Top with the parmesan and breadcrumbs
10. Put the tin back into your oven for half an hour
11. Allow to rest and cool for 15 minutes
12. Serve with crusty bread

Rainbow Tabbouleh

Colorful and quick, this tabbouleh recipe is a one tin dish that is packed with delicious and fresh ingredients. When cooked with tomatoes, the bulgur wheat in this dish develops a truly wonderful flavor, while the appearance is elegant and beautiful – ideal for serving in its roasting tin. Whether you're ready to eat more plant-based foods for health reasons or whether you're trying to impress a vegan friend, this is the ideal meal for any time of the year.

Serves 2

Preparation time – 15 minutes

Cooking time – 20 minutes

Total time – 35 minutes

Ingredients

- 200g//1 ½ cups bulgur wheat
- 250ml// 1 cup of vegetable stock
- 6 chopped vine tomatoes
- Juice and the zest of a lemon
- 25g// ¼ cup of chopped fresh coriander
- 50g// ½ cup of chopped fresh parsley
- 1 tablespoon of extra virgin olive oil
- Black pepper to taste
- 1 teaspoon of sea salt
- 4 sliced spring onions
- 6 sliced radishes

- ◆ 1 sliced avocado
- ◆ Seeds of 1 pomegranate

Instructions

1. Preheat your oven to 200C//400F
2. Mix the stock with the bulgur wheat, lemon zest and tomatoes in the roasting tin
3. Put the tin in the oven
4. Cook uncovered for 20 minutes
5. Remove the tin from the oven
6. Stir well
7. Allow to steam dry for five minutes
8. Stir the coriander, the lemon juice, the olive oil, parsley, pepper and salt through the bulgur wheat
9. Stir the radishes and spring onions into the bulgur wheat
10. Top with the pomegranate seeds and the avocado
11. Serve warm

Chickpea, Coconut And Beetroot Curry

When you're looking for a simple yet spicy midweek meal for the vegans in your life, this easy one-tin recipe is warming, exotic and delicious. It's also incredibly colorful thanks to the beetroot, and when served with naan bread or rice, it creates a wonderfully satisfying meal for any occasion. This Asian-inspired dinner is sure to impress thanks to its sophisticated appearance, but it's a breeze to put together, with the coconut milk effortlessly reducing down into a tasty and simple curry sauce.

Serves 2

Preparation time – 15 minutes

Cooking time – 50 minutes

Total time – 1 hour 5 minutes

Ingredients

- 1 chopped onion
- 600g//4 cups peeled, cut beetroot
- 1 can of drained chickpeas
- 2 crushed garlic cloves
- 1 chopped red chilli
- 1 teaspoon of ground coriander
- 1 teaspoon of ground cumin
- A teaspoon of ground ginger
- ½ teaspoon of ground turmeric
- 1 teaspoon of sea salt

- 1 tablespoon of vegetable oil
- 1 can of coconut milk
- Coconut flakes, fresh coriander, naan bread and basmati rice to serve

Instructions

1. Preheat your oven to 200C//400 F
2. Mix the chickpeas, beetroot and onion in your roasting tin together with the ginger, the garlic, spices, chilli, salt and oil
3. Put the tin in the oven
4. Cook for 40 minutes
5. Stir the coconut milk
6. Pour the coconut milk over the vegetables and chickpeas
7. Mix well
8. Put the tin back in the oven
9. Cook for 10 minutes
10. Season with salt then scatter with coconut flakes and coriander
11. Serve with naan breads and rice

Crisp Tamarind Sprouts With Shallots And Peanuts

Whether you're looking for a great way to jazz up sprouts to accompany your Christmas dinner or whether you're searching for a healthy and vegan midweek meal you can prepare in minutes, this tasty dinner that takes its inspiration from Indian street food is sure to tick all your boxes. Combining sprouts with crispy chickpeas and tamarind dressing, this dish is ideal when served with puffed rice as a snack or with naan breads and yogurt as a satisfying entrée.

Serves 4

Preparation time – 10 minutes

Cooking time – 25 minutes

Total time – 35 minutes

Ingredients

- 500g//5 1/3 cups halved Brussels sprouts
- 200g//2 cups halved and peeled banana shallots
- 1 can of drained chickpeas
- 1 teaspoon of ground cumin
- 1 teaspoon of ground coriander
- 1 teaspoon of chilli powder
- 2 tablespoons of vegetable oil
- A tablespoon of tamarind paste
- 1 teaspoon of brown sugar
- 2 teaspoons of sea salt
- 20g// ¼ cup chopped salted peanuts

- A handful of chopped fresh coriander
- 1 teaspoon of mango powder
- 1 teaspoon of chaat masala
- 4 tablespoons coconut flavor yogurt
- Naan bread to serve

Instructions

1. Preheat your oven to 200C//400F
2. Mix the shallots, sprouts, chickpeas, salt, 1 tablespoon of oil and the spices together in your roasting tin
3. Put in the oven
4. Cook for 25 minutes
5. Meanwhile, mix the sugar, tamarind paste and a tablespoon of the oil together
6. Toss the cooked vegetables with the prepared dressing
7. Scatter the coriander, peanuts, mango powder and chaat masala over the top
8. Serve with yogurt and naan breads

Roast Root Vegetable Bake

A simple vegan dish to eat as a standalone entrée or as a side dish, this vegetable bake is hearty, filling and, above all, nutritious. Even the most hardened meat eater in the family is sure to love the rich flavors of this midweek vegan meal and if you're preparing this for non-vegan diners, why not add a little feta cheese for even more delicious taste?

Serves 4

Preparation time – 15 minutes

Cooking time – 50 minutes

Total time – 1 hour 5 minutes

Ingredients

- 1kg//2 lbs of mixed root vegetables including swede, parsnips and carrots, halved and cut up into sticks
- 220g//1 1/3 cups of halved new potatoes
- 3 garlic cloves with the skin left on
- 4 sprigs of rosemary
- 2 tablespoons of olive oil
- 4 sprigs of thyme
- 50g//1/4 cup of snacking seeds or nuts
- Optional 50g//1 cup of feta cheese
- 2 tablespoons of olive oil
- Juice of 1 lemon

- ◆ A handful of chopped parsley

Instructions

1. Preheat the oven to 200C//400F
2. Put the root vegetables, the potatoes and cloves of garlic into your roasting tin
3. Nestle the herbs amongst them
4. Drizzle olive oil over the top
5. Ross well to coat everything thoroughly
6. Season to suit your taste
7. Put the tin into the oven
8. Cook for 50 minutes
9. Remove from the oven
10. Take the garlic out of the tin
11. Squeeze it out of its skin
12. Blitz the garlic in your blender along with the lemon juice, the parsley and two tablespoons of olive oil toprepare the dressing
13. Pour the dressing over the vegetables
14. Scatter the nuts and feta cheese if using over the top
15. Serve warm

Healthy Single Roasting Tin Recipes

More people than ever before these days are putting their health and well-being first when it comes to everyday eating. Obesity is an increasing problem, so it's no wonder that there's a renewed interest in pursuing healthier options and choosing foods that won't pile on the pounds.

The good news is that it's possible to create nutritious and healthy meals without a lot of fuss. Some people believe that healthy = complicated, however, this couldn't be further from the truth. Rather, there are plenty of great recipes that you can easily prepare in your home kitchen using healthy ingredients that will keep you satisfied and feeling full but without spending hours preparing and stirring.

These single roasting tin healthy recipes will help you to stay at your ideal weight while also ensuring that every family member enjoys a satisfying dinner, whether or not they're on a diet.

Chicken Fajitas In A Roasting Tin

If you thought that the only way to prepare fajitas was to sweat over a hot stove you'll be delighted to discover this single roasting tin recipe. Making it quicker and easier than ever before to prepare this Mexican inspired classic, you can whip up your dinner in just half an hour– perfect for a midweek supper or as part of a larger south of the border feast.

Serves 4

Preparation time – 15 minutes

Cooking time – 18 minutes

Total time – 33 minutes

Ingredients

- 2 teaspoons of chilli powder
- 1 ½ teaspoons of ground cumin
- 1 teaspoon of ground paprika
- ½ teaspoon of ground coriander
- Black pepper and salt to taste
- 680g//1 ½ lbs of chicken breasts (without skin or bones) sliced in strips
- A sliced red pepper
- 1 sliced yellow pepper
- 1 sliced green pepper
- 1 sliced onion
- 2 minced garlic cloves

- ◆ 3 tablespoons of chopped coriander
- ◆ 2 tablespoons of lime juice
- ◆ 3 tablespoons of olive oil
- ◆ 8 flour tortillas
- ◆ Sour cream, guacamole, avocado slices, diced tomatoes, and some grated cheese to serve

Instructions

1 Preheat your oven to 200C//400F

2 Spray the roasting tin with a non-stick cooking spray

3 Mix the chilli powder, the cumin, the coriander, paprika, flakes of salt and ground pepper into a bowl and set aside

4 Spread the onion and the peppers in the roasting tin

5 Place the chicken breast strips on top of the vegetables

6 Sprinkle seasoning and the garlic over them evenly

7 Drizzle the olive oil generously over the top

8 Toss to coat evenly

9 Ensure that there is only a single layer of chicken and vegetables

10 Place your tin in the oven

11 Cook for 25 minutes, tossing partway through

12 Warm the tortillas in foil during the final five minutes of cooking the fajita filling

13 Remove the fajita filling from the oven and drizzle the lime juice over the top

14 Add some salt to suit your taste

15 Serve in the warm tortillas along with all the toppings

Tofu With Chickpeas And Vegetables

Whether you're on a diet yourself, looking for a vegetarian option that is also healthy and extremely nutritious, or whether you're just looking for inspiration for an unexpectedly filling dinner that's quick and simple to prepare and that contains no meat, this single roasting tin dinner offers you plenty of lean protein and lots of delicious flavor.

Serves 2

Preparation time – 15 minutes

Cooking time – 35 minutes

Total time – 50 minutes

Ingredients

- 225g//8oz of tofu, cubed
- 2 tablespoons of olive oil
- ½ teaspoon of curry powder
- 300g//1 ½ cups of canned, drained chickpeas
- Salt and pepper to taste
- 1 large bulb of fennel, cored and wedged
- 20 halved cherry tomatoes
- 1 bunch of asparagus with the woody ends trimmed

Instructions

1 Preheat the oven to 200C//400F
2 Line the roasting pan with some baking paper
3 Spread the cubes of tofu on a kitchen towel
4 Cover the tofu with another kitchen towel
5 Press down to remove the moisture
6 Whisk the oil, curry powder, pepper and salt together in bowl
7 Add the chickpeas and tofu
8 Toss well to coat the tofu and chickpeas in the dressing
9 Spread the chickpeas and tofu in the roasting tin evenly
10 Add the fennel
11 Roast for 20 minutes
12 Add asparagus and tomatoes to the tin
13 Season with pepper and salt
14 Return to your oven for a further 15 minutes
15 Cool for 5 minutes
16 Serve

Lentil And Aubergine Layered Bake

This vegetarian dish is quick and simple to prepare and minimizes your washing up since it requires just a single roasting tin. Comforting on a winter evening, or light and tasty when served with salad and crusty bread as a summer entrée, this versatile meal is sure to satisfy even the most committed meat eater.

Serves 4

Preparation time – 15 minutes

Cooking time – 45 minutes

Total time –1 hour

Ingredients

- 2 aubergines cut into long slices
- 3 tablespoons of olive oil
- 140g// 2/3 cup puy lentils
- 2 chopped onions
- 3 chopped cloves garlic
- 300g//2 cups butternut squash (cooked)
- A can of chopped tomatoes
- A handful of basil leaves
- 125g//1 cup of torn mozzarella cheese

Instructions

1 Preheat the oven to 200C//400F

2 Brush each of the sides of each aubergine slice with oil

3 Put the aubergine slices in the roasting tin

4 Season to taste

5 Cook for 20 minutes turning once

6 Cook the lentils

7 Heat up the oil in your frying pan

8 Put the garlic and onions in the pan

9 Cook until soft

10 Stir through all the tomatoes and squash along with half the can of water

11 Simmer for 15 minutes to thicken the sauce

12 Stir the lentils, seasoning and basil into your sauce

13 Spoon a lentil layer into the roasting tin

14 Topwith slices ofaubergine

15 Repeat ending with an aubergine layer

16 Scatter the mozzarella cheese on top

17 Cook for 15 minutes

18 Serve hot

Curry Chicken with New Potatoes

Healthy yet satisfying, this chicken roasting tin dish uses classic Indian spices to produce a lightly spiced meal that's perfect for a simple family supper. Quick and easy to prepare, it brings a little Asian-inspired flavor to any evening meal without adding too many calories.

Serves 4

Preparation time – 15 minutes

Cooking time – 45 minutes (plus marinating time)

Total time – 1 hour

Ingredients

- 8 chicken drumsticks
- 3 tablespoons of olive oil
- 1 teaspoon of garlic paste
- 1 teaspoon of ginger paste
- 1 teaspoonof garam masala
- 1teaspoon of turmeric
- 150ml//1 ½ cups of natural yogurt
- 500g//3 1/3 cups of halved new potatoes

- 4 chopped tomatoes
- 1 chopped red onion
- A handful of coriander chopped

Instructions

1   Put the chicken drumsticks into a bowl

2   Add 1 tablespoon of oil along with the garlic, garam masala, ginger, turmeric and 2 tablespoons of yogurt

3   Use your hands and mix well together and to coat the chicken

4   Allow to marinate for half an hour (or in your refrigerator overnight)

5   Preheat the oven to 160C//325F

6   Put the new potatoes into a roasting tin

7   Add the rest of the oil and seasoning

8   Add the drumsticks

9   Cook for 45 minutes

10 Scatter the onion, tomatoes, seasoning and coriander over the top

11 Serve with the remainder of the yogurt on the side

Tomato Baked Eggs

Perhaps you're looking for a light meal to enjoy at the end of a busy day, or maybe you're looking for a speedy brunch dish to celebrate the weekend that won't cause you to gain weight. Either way, these tomato baked eggs are quick and easy to prepare, simple to cook and are delicious, especially when served with slices of crusty bread. Even the pickiest of eaters is sure to enjoy dining on this deceptively simple entrée.

Serves 4

Preparation time – 10 minutes

Cooking time – 50 minutes

Total time – 1 hour

Ingredients

◆ 12 ripe vine tomatoes

◆ 3 cloves of garlic

◆ 3 tablespoons of olive oil

◆ 4 large eggs

◆ 2 tablespoons of chopped parsley

Instructions

1 Preheat your oven to 200C//400F

2 Cut up the tomatoes into thick wedges or quarters

3 Spread the tomatoes over the base of a roasting tin

4 Peel and slice the garlic

5 Sprinkle the garlic over the tomatoes

6 Add olive oil

7 Season with pepper and salt

8 Stir everything to coat the tomatoes well

9 Put the tin in the oven

10 Cook for 40 minutes

11 Make four spaces in the tomatoes

12 Break one egg into each of the gaps

13 Cover up the tin with tin foil

14 Put the tin back into the oven

15 Cook for 10 minutes to set the eggs

16 Scatter the herbs over the top

17 Serve hot with toast, green salad or warm ciabatta

Single Roasting Tin Snacks And Desserts

At the end of a long day at work, who doesn't want to settle down in front of the TV with a tasty snack while you wait for dinner to cook? Or who wouldn't relish the opportunity to indulge in a wonderfully decadent dessert after the evening meal?

However, with a lack of time to prepare complex treats, it can be tempting to simply pop to the store and buy pre-packaged products which are often loaded with unhealthy ingredients and which are often expensive. Luckily, thanks to your humble roasting tin, you can make your own delicious snacks and desserts that are simple and speedy to make but that satisfy your sweet tooth wonderfully.

You may never have thought about using your roasting tin for anything other than a joint of meat, but rest assured, this kitchen staple can work wonders when it comes to preparing sweet snacks and desserts that round off any meal perfectly.

Vanilla Cake

You may never have thought about making a cake in a roasting pan, but rest assured, it's perfectly possible. In fact, not only is it possible, it's actually extremely effective! You can make a large traybake style cake that will serve a lot of people at once, or that will make lots of little snacks to enjoy over the course of a few days! This classic vanilla cake is a breeze to whip up, and it's sure to satisfy even the sweetest tooth, either as a tasty after-dinner treat or as an indulgent snack to take to work or school.

Serves 20

Preparation time – 15 minutes

Cooking time – 40 minutes

Total time – 55 minutes

Ingredients

- 5 eggs
- 450g//2 ¼ cups granulated sugar
- 300g//1 ¾ cups of plain flour
- 1 tablespoon baking powder

- 175ml// ¾ cup of boiling water
- 125g//1 cup chopped hazelnuts
- 250g//1 cup margarine or butter
- 200ml//1 cup milk
- 50g// ½ cup vanilla sugar

Instructions

1. Preheat your oven to 200C//400F
2. Grease your roasting tin
3. Dust it lightly with flour
4. Whisk up the sugar and the eggs together until they're fluffy and light
5. Combine the baking powder with the plain flour
6. Fold into your egg mixture
7. Add the hot water to the mix
8. Pour the whole mixture into your roasting tin
9. Sprinkle the nuts over the top
10. Bake for 40 minutes on the middle shelf of your oven
11. Remove and cool
12. Meanwhile, put the milk and margarine/butter in a pan
13. Boil for 2 minutes on a high heat
14. Add the vanilla sugar to the pan
15. Cut the cake in two layers
16. Soak both layers with the margarine/butter and the milk mixture
17. Sandwich the layers of the cake together
18. Ensure the chopped nuts layer is on top
19. Serve plain or with some fresh berries and whipped cream for an indulgent dessert

Roast Pineapple With Pistachios And Honey

Perhaps you're looking for the ideal way to round off a light meal, or maybe you're looking for a sticky and delicious dessert that's quick and simple to make? This delicious and indulgent one tin dish takes all of the hard work out of making sweet treats and it packs plenty of exotic flavor. The ideal end to a Greek or Caribbean-inspired dinner, this dessert is equally good as a sweet treat in its own right.

Serves 4

Preparation time – 10 minutes

Cooking time – 40 minutes

Total time – 50 minutes

Ingredients

- 50g// ½ cup dark brown sugar
- 125ml// ½ cup orange juice
- 3 tablespoons of honey
- 1 pineapple, cored, peeled then cut up into 8 wedges lengthways
- 125g//¼ cup of yogurt or crème fraiche
- 50g// 1/3 cup unsalted natural pistachios, chopped
- 2 tablespoons fresh mint leaves

Instructions

1. Preheat your oven to 230C//450F
2. Line a roasting tin with baking paper
3. Stir the sugar, juice and honey together in your bowl
4. Stir until all of the sugar has completely dissolved
5. Add the pineapple to the bowl then toss well in the mix to coat evenly
6. Allow to marinate, occasionally tossing, for ten minutes
7. Put the pineapple in the tin, with one flat side facing downwards
8. Save the rest of the marinade for later
9. Cook the pineapple for 15 minutes
10. Turn the tin then brush with the remaining marinade
11. Cook under caramelized and tender for around 15 minutes
12. Drizzle the rest of the marinade over the top
13. Allow to cool down slightly
14. Spoon the crème fraiche or yogurt alongside the pineapple
15. Sprinkle the mint and nuts on top
16. Serve warm

Plum Tarts With Black Pepper And Honey

Super simple to prepare, this is the ideal dessert to impress friends and family when they call around unexpectedly for dinner! Easy to make, using ingredients that work perfectly together, this is a tasty treat to complement any meal, and these tarts also make a wonderful snack between meals!

Serves 6

Preparation time – 10 minutes

Cooking time – 30 minutes

Total time – 40 minutes

Ingredients

- 1 sheet of ready-rolled puff pastry
- 450g/1 lb pitted plums cut in wedges
- 50g//¼ cup of sugar
- Black pepper to taste
- 1 tablespoon of honey
- Sea salt to taste

Instructions

1   Preheat your oven to 220C//425F

2   Cut the pastry up into six squares

3   Line the roasting tin with parchment paper

4   Place the pastry squares on the parchment paper

5   Prick the prepared pastry with the prongs of a fork all over

6   Place the plums atop the pastry

7   Leave a border of ½"

8   Sprinkle sugar over the top

9   Add grinds of black pepper on top

10   Put the tin into the oven and cook for 30 minutes, turning partway through

11   Take out of the oven

12   Drizzle honey over the top

13   Sprinkle the salt over the top

14   Serve warm

Cookie Bars

The ultimate take anywhere snack, these cookie bars are packed with delicious store cupboard ingredients such as peanut butter and oats along with indulgent chocolate chips for a tasty treat at any time of day. Perfect for lunch boxes, for snacking in front of the TV or even as a casual dessert, these bars will satisfy adults and kids alike!

Serves 36

Preparation time – 15 minutes

Cooking time – 20 minutes

Total time – 35 minutes

Ingredients

- 4 eggs
- 250g// 1 ½ cups of sugar
- 200g//1 cup of brown sugar
- 1 tablespoon of vanilla extract
- ¾ teaspoon of salt
- 480g//2 cups of crunchy or creamy peanut butter
- 5 tablespoons of butter
- 500g//18oz of rolled oats
- 2 ½ teaspoons of baking soda
- 350g//2 cups of chocolate chips

Instructions

1. Place a rack in the center of your oven and preheat it to 180C//350F
2. Butter a roasting tin and set aside
3. Using an electric mixer or spoon, mix the sugars and eggs together in a bowl
4. Beat the vanilla, salt, butter and peanut butter together until smooth
5. Stir the baking soda into the mix, making sure there are no lumps
6. Add the oats and chocolate chips
7. Spread the batter in the roasting tin
8. Press down and smooth the top so it isan even layer
9. Bake for 22 minutes
10. Leave to cool
11. Slice and serve

Easy Rice Pudding

Is there any more classic dessert than a traditional rice pudding? This single roasting tin recipe is the ultimate comfort food for anyone who wants a warming dessert at the end of a long day. Quick and simple to prepare, the oven does all the hard work of cooking the rice while you can enjoy a little relaxation time.

Serves 4

Preparation time – 5 minutes

Cooking time -2 hours

Total time – 2 hours 5 minutes

Ingredients

- 100g// ½ cup of pudding (short grain) rice
- 50g// ½ cup of sugar
- 350ml//1 ½ cups of milk
- 350ml/1 ½ cups of cream
- Pinch of nutmeg

Instructions

1. Preheat the oven to 200C//400F
2. Add the rice, sugar, milk, cream and nutmeg to the roasting tin
3. Mix well
4. Cover with tin foil
5. Put the tin in the oven
6. Cook for 2 hours
7. Serve with a dollop of your favorite jam for a touch of extra luxury

Bread And Butter Pudding

Another classic dessert that can easily be prepared in your favorite roasting tin is a bread and butter pudding. Filling, satisfying and wonderfully comforting, especially on a cold winter's evening, this family friendly dessert is one of the most popular ways of using up stale bread and it's sure to keep every member of the family happy.

> Serves 4
>
> Preparation time - 30 minutes
>
> Cooking time – 45 minutes
>
> Total time – 1 hour 15 minutes

Ingredients

- ◆ 25g//1 oz of butter
- ◆ 50g//2 oz of sultanas
- ◆ 8 slices of white bread
- ◆ 350ml/12 fl oz full fat milk
- ◆ 2 teaspoons of cinnamon powder
- ◆ 50ml/ 2 fl oz of double cream
- ◆ Two medium eggs
- ◆ 25g//1 oz sugar

- ◆ Grated nutmeg to taste

Instructions

1. Grease the roasting tin with the butter
2. Cut the bread crusts off and spread each of the slices with butter
3. Cut the slices into triangles
4. Place a layer of buttered bread slices in the tin with the buttered side facing upwards
5. Sprinkle some sultanas over the bread
6. Sprinkle some cinnamon over the top
7. Repeat this simple process until all the bread is fully used up
8. Set aside
9. Warm the cream and milk gently in a pan to scalding point over a low heat
10. Avoid boiling the mix
11. Whisk the sugar and eggs together in a bowl until pale
12. Add the mixture of the milk and the cream while it's still warm
13. Stir well
14. Pour the mixture through a sieve into the bowl
15. Add the mixture over the layered bread
16. Sprinkle on the remainder of the sugar and nutmeg
17. Allow to sit for half an hour
18. Put the tin in your oven for around 45 minutes
19. Serve hot or cold

Apple Crumble

Incredibly simple to prepare, this is the ultimate cheat's dessert when you simply don't have enough time to cook but need a sweet treat that complements your meal. Ready to pop in the oven in minutes, this is a dessert classic that will satisfy your sweet tooth and will take you back to your grandmother's kitchen!

Serves 4

Preparation time – 15 minutes

Cooking time – 40 minutes

Total time – 55 minutes

Ingredients

- 2 cans of cooked apple pie filling
- 2 tablespoons of caster sugar
- 175g//1 ¼ cups plain flour
- 110g// ½ cup caster sugar
- 110g// ½ cup cubed cold butter
- 1 tablespoon of rolled oats
- 1 tablespoon of demerara sugar

Instructions

1. Preheat your oven to 200C//400F
2. Mix the apple pie filling with two tablespoons of caster sugar
3. Put the mix into a roasting tin
4. Flatten the mix so that it is evenly spread
5. Mix the remaining caster sugar and flour in a bowl
6. Add butter to the flour and sugar mix and rub it until it looks like fine breadcrumbs
7. Pour the breadcrumb mix over the apples
8. Smooth into an even layer
9. Sprinkle the demerara sugar and oats over the top
10. Put the tin into the oven
11. Cook for 40 minutes
12. Serve hot with cream, custard or ice cream

A Final Word

Hopefully, the recipes in this book have shown you that it's possible to use your trusty old roasting tin to make a lot more than just your Christmas turkey! Whenever you need a classic meat dish, a fish supper, or a vegan or vegetarian main meal that requires very little effort, you can be confident that your roasting tin is the ideal solution. Simply throw in a few ingredients and let the oven take the strain – you can enjoy the freedom that it gives you to spend some quality time with your family, something that is all too precious in this busy modern era.

We hope that we've inspired you to create amazing entrees and desserts in your own kitchen using just a single roasting tin. You can also use these recipes as a base to create your own delicious dinners. Enjoy cooking!

Printed in Great Britain
by Amazon